Snow White

Key sound aw spellings: a, au, augh, aw, ough
Secondary sounds: igh, ake, nd

Written by Nick Page
Illustrated by Clare Fennell

Princess Snow White, skin like snow,
had a stepmom, long ago.
Every night, this queen would call
to her mirror on the wall:

"Mirror, mirror, on the wall,
who's the fairest of them all?"

The mirror says, "I speak true,
fairest of them all is you."

Snow White grows up
fair and kind.
One day, Queenie
speaks her mind,
**"Mirror, mirror,
on the wall,
who is the fairest
of them all?"**

The mirror says,
"I speak right.
Fairest of them all?
Snow White."

Queenie's heart goes cold as water.
She sends a man to kill her daughter.
He takes Snow White to the wood
but lets her go: his heart is good.

7

In the woods, she finds Small Hall,
a house for someone not very tall.
She calls "hello," then knocks at the door.
But no one's home. "Shall I explore?"

Hello!

Stay!

Stay!

Tired, she falls asleep in a chair.
Seven dwarfs come in. "Who's that there?"
She tells her story and they say, "Right!
stay in Small Hall, if you like."

9

Back at court, a week goes by.
Queenie gives her normal cry:
"Mirror, mirror, on the wall,
who's the fairest of them all?"

The mirror says, "You're all right,
alternatively, there's Snow White."

Queenie bawls and Queenie roars,
"Still alive! Well, this means war!"

She chants a spell and then – surprise!
She's small and old – a great disguise!
Grabs her cloak and shawl and more,
a rosy apple with poisonous core.
Finds Small Hall and there's Snow White!
"Try my apple – take a bite!"

She snorts with glee, as Snow White falls:
"Now I'm the fairest of them all!"

When the dwarfs came home, they found
Snow White lying on the ground.

How they cried – they all adored her.

They built a coffin and, in it, stored her.

Back at court, the queen transforms,
and takes again her usual form.
"Mirror, mirror, on the wall,
who's the fairest of them all?"

The mirror sighs, "You're fairest of fair.
Snow White's gone – what more do I care?"

A prince rides by and sees Snow White.
"She must be mine!"
(It's love at first sight.)

They lift the coffin, then they stumble
and out of her mouth, the apple tumbles.
A yawn. A stretch. She lifts her head.
She's reborn! Snow White's not dead!

Meanwhile, Queenie has a thought –
she asks the mirror to report:
**"Mirror, mirror, on the wall,
who's the fairest of them all?"**

The mirror says, "Cue applause,
it's Snow White! She shoots! She scores!"

The queen goes mad, she turns all red,
her hair falls out, she drops down dead.

The prince asked Snow White for her hand
and all the dwarfs, a song they sang.
"Mirror, mirror, on the wall,
who's the fairest of them all?"

The mirror said, "I speak right,
fairest of all is, forever, Snow White."

Key sound

There are several different groups of letters that make the aw sound. Read the words and use them in questions for the magic mirrors. For example: Mirror, mirror, on the wall, will I ever go to a ball? What do you think the mirror would reply?

fall
wall
all
ball
small
hall
tall

fought

nought

thought

bought

yawn
shawl
bawled
scrawled
straw

naughty
daughter
caught
taught

pause
cause
applause

Letters together

Look at these groups of letters and say the sounds they make.

igh **ake** **nd**

Follow the words that contain **igh** to help Snow White find love at first sight.

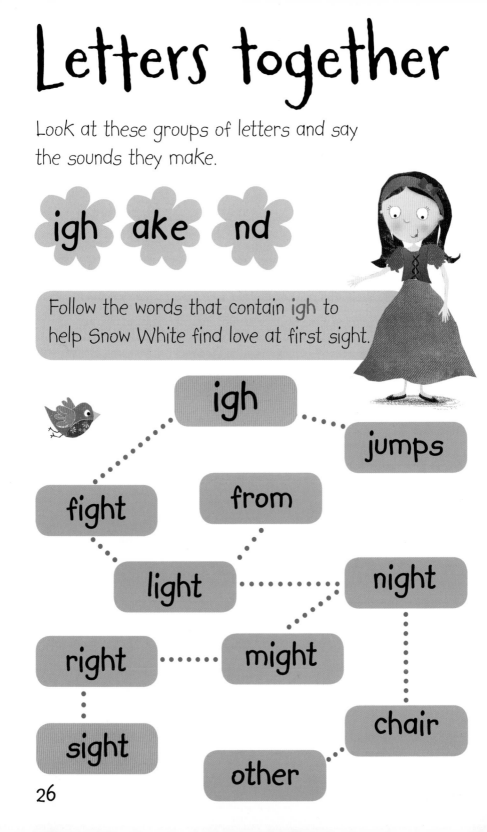

igh

jumps

fight

from

light

night

right

might

sight

chair

other

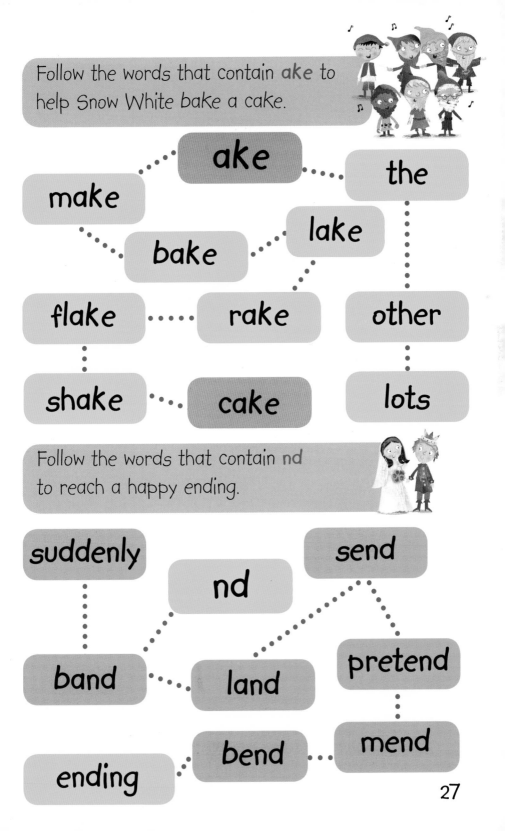

Follow the words that contain **ake** to help Snow White bake a cake.

ake

make

the

lake

bake

flake

rake

other

shake

cake

lots

Follow the words that contain **nd** to reach a happy ending.

suddenly

send

nd

band

land

pretend

ending

bend

mend

27

Rhyming words

Read the words in the flowers and point to other words that rhyme with them.

kind		low
grow	**snow**	wall

apple		seen
shawl	**queen**	been

ball		tall
mirror	**wall**	home

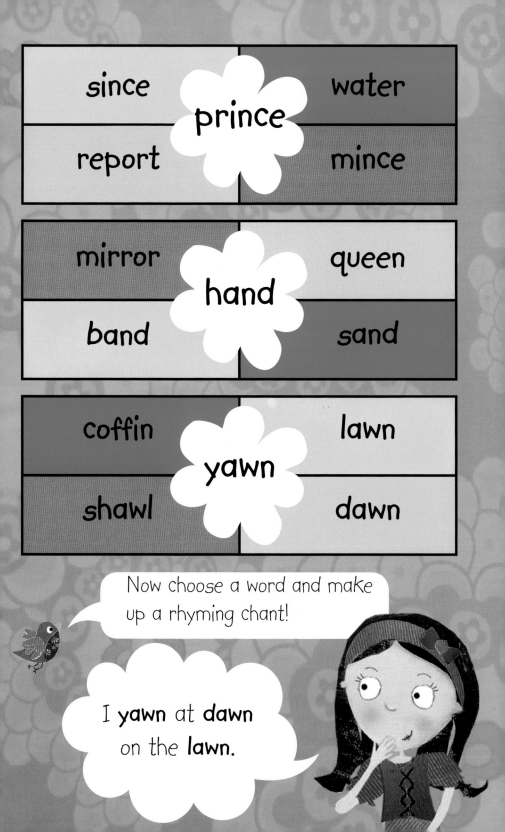

since

water

prince

report

mince

mirror

queen

hand

band

sand

coffin

lawn

yawn

shawl

dawn

Now choose a word and make up a rhyming chant!

I **yawn** at **dawn** on the **lawn**.

Sight words

Many common words can be difficult to sound out.
Practice them by reading these sentences about
the story. Now make more sentences using other
sight words from
around the border.

A **man** took
Snow White to
the woods.

Snow White lived
with the dwarfs.

The queen **asked**
her mirror who was
the fairest of all.

Snow White
and the prince
had a party.

because • they

• trees • bad • tea • eyes • white • looks • dark • looking